Exhibit '64
OLD DOGS LEARNING NEW TRICKS

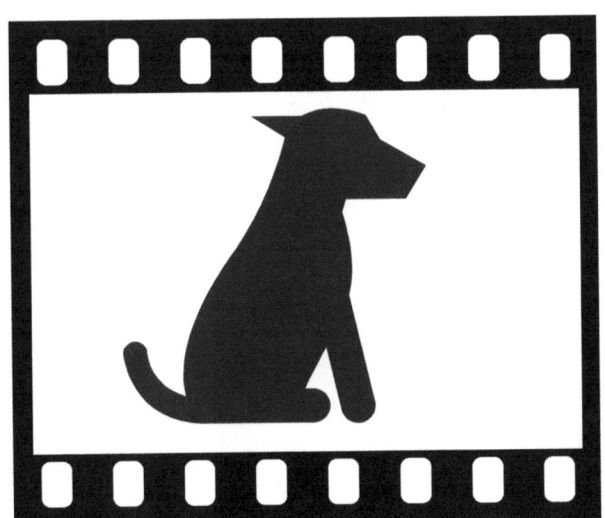 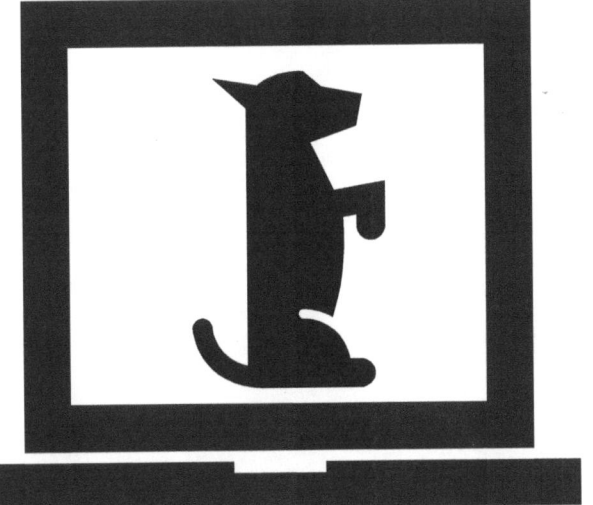

From Film to Digital 1964-2014

"The machine in photography is only a misunderstood tool. A picture can only be made when the mind is aware of the facts of the media, before commanding the manipulation of the elements."

1964 *Techmila*

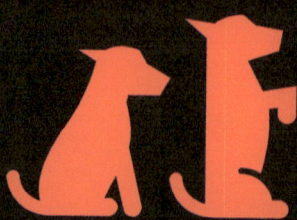

INTRODUCTION

"Similarities and differences" is the dance we do as professionals in the visual arts. As students we learned about photography from the inside out. Professors Arnold, White, Todd, Zakia, Shoemaker, Rickmers, Stroebel, Smith, and many more drummed the science and mechanics of photography into our heads during lectures and labs. These men formed the structural foundation that made RIT the bell weather of photographic education.

The flood of information about the medium laid the groundwork for the professional careers we chose to follow. The scope of those careers is evidenced in the backgrounds of the 14 individuals presented here.

As the tsunami of change from silver based imaging to the pixel based systems overtook us, we were faced with analyzing the "similarities and differences" between the two and applying these changes to our work.

Some work stayed the same, only the camera and substrate changed, while others took a more radical approach, using the new technology in ways never dreamed of in 1964.

BARLEY, WILLIAM B., Charlotte, N.C.
(Photography) Sigma Phi;
Ski Club; *Reporter*, Editor-in-Chief

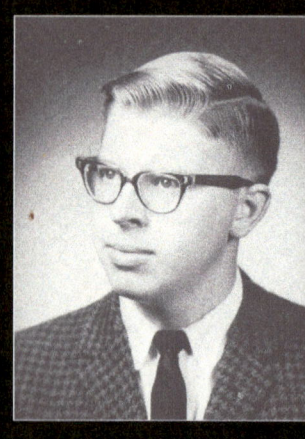

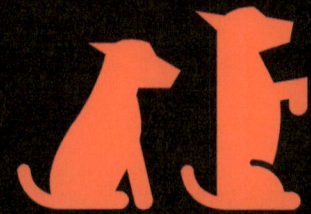

BILL **BARLEY**

Bachelor of Fine Arts

After graduation Bill moved to Columbia, SC to pursue a career at *The State Record* Newspaper. After 18 months he left the paper and began a very successful career in commercial advertising and freelance photojournalism.
In the late '70's Bill turned to aviation and through the use of his own plane was able to expand the geographic range of his client base doing annual reports, brochures, aerial and architectural assignments. Working through the digital evolution he is now supporting the regional art community with high-quality canvas and fine art paper printing through Studio BB&A.

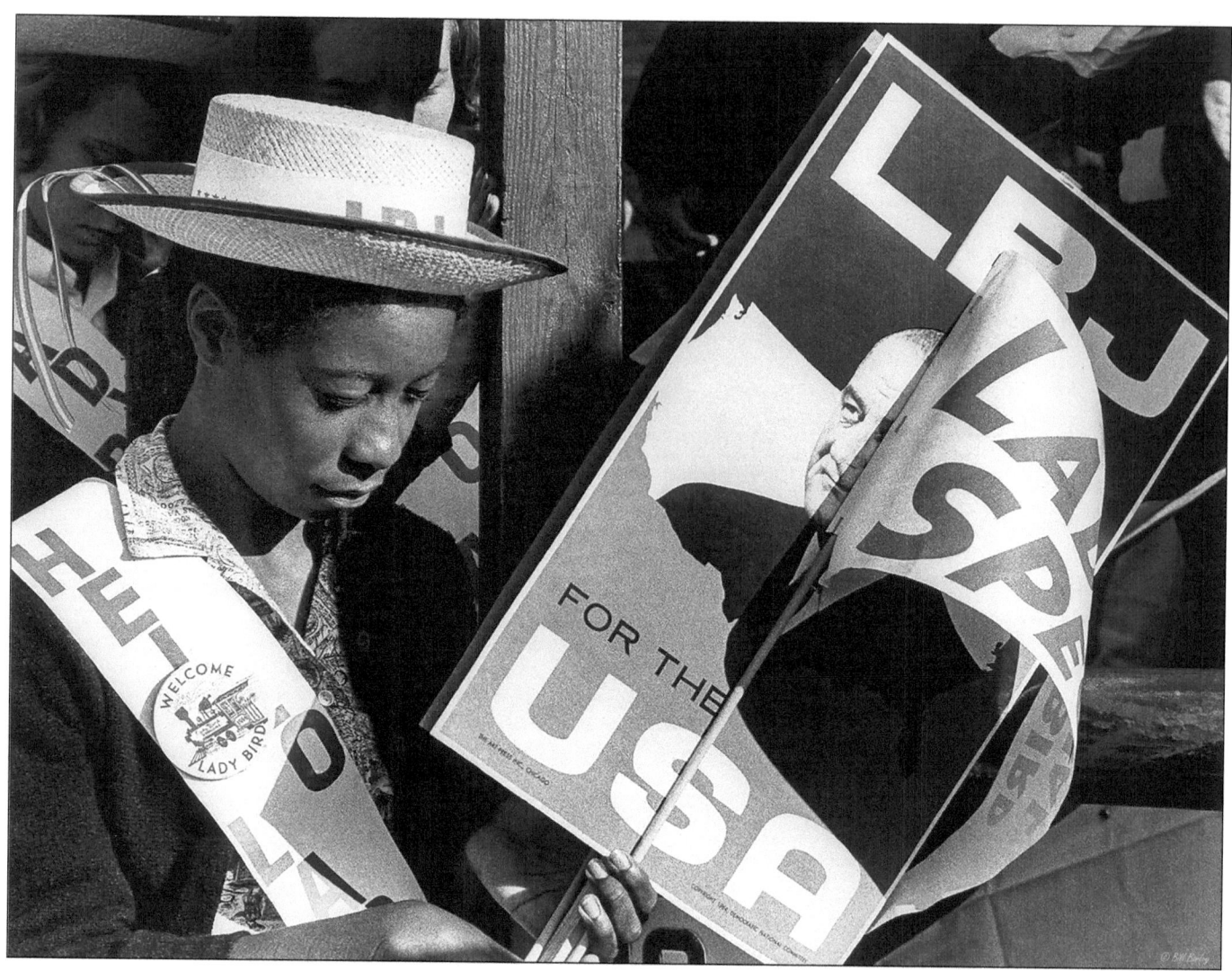

FILM

LBJ Campaigner, October, 1965

Campaign Worker for Lyndon Johnson during Lady Bird
Johnson's southern "Lady Bird Special" train tour.

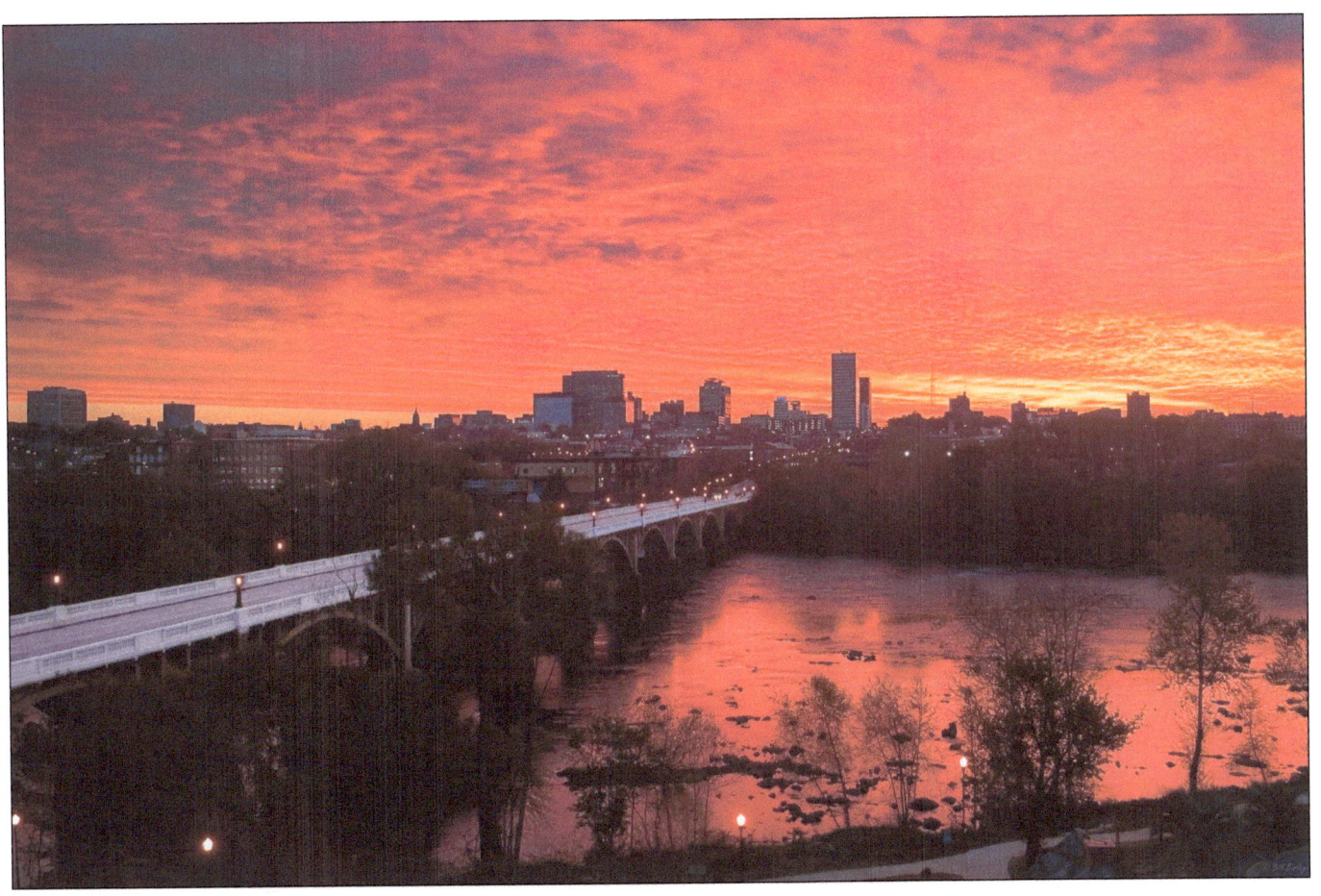

DIGITAL

Vista Dawn

Gervais St. Bridge at the Congaree River, Columbia, SC

BEARD, LLOYD E., Chicago, Illinois
(Photography) Delta Lamda Epsion;
Student Council; SCF; Reporter

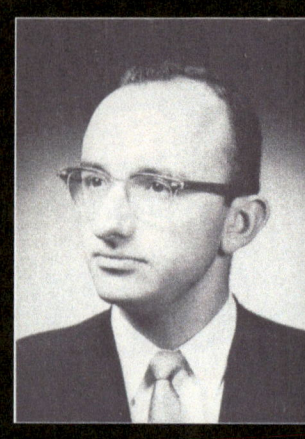

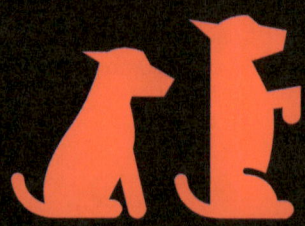

LLOYD **BEARD**

Bachelor of Fine Arts

Throughout his career Lloyd has worked in industrial and photographic laboratories. He has worked for Xerox, NCR, and other corporations as a photographer and photo lab technician. Lloyd and his wife have owned and operated several commercial photography businesses eventually landing in Birmingham, Alabama.

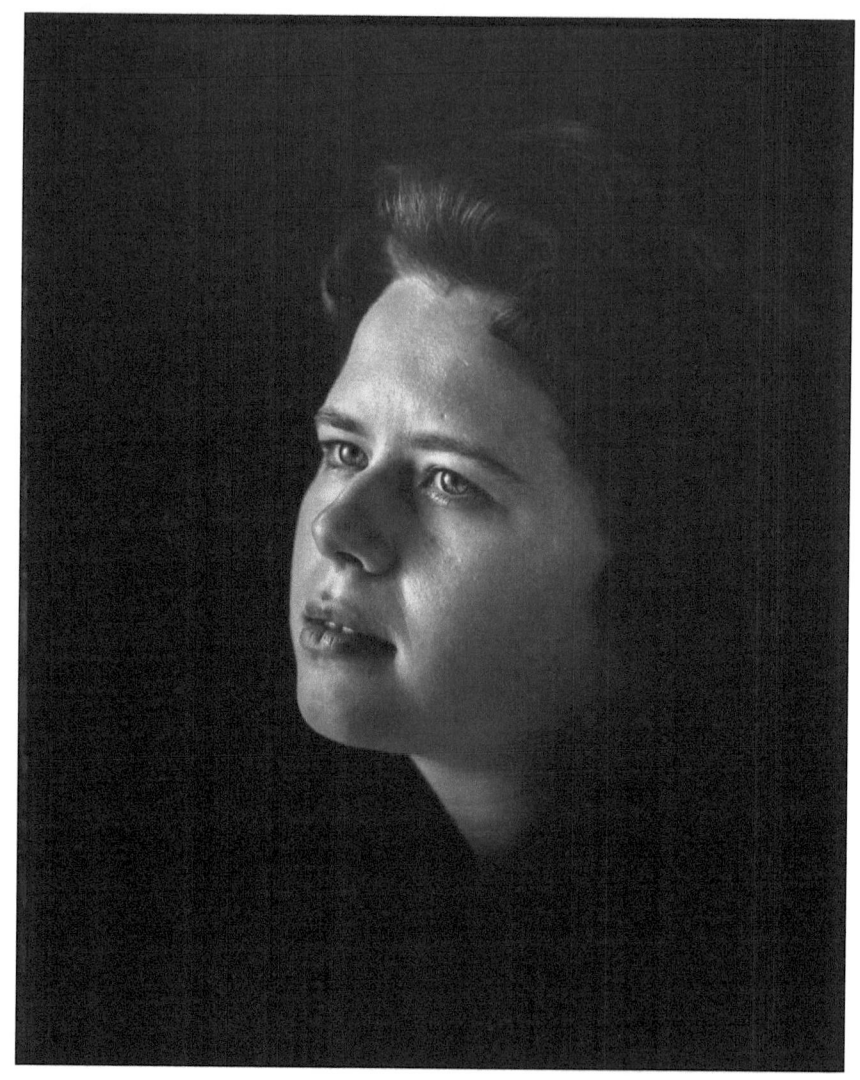

FILM

My True Love – A portrait of Lloyd's wife

4x5 black & white negative material, printed on fiber based paper

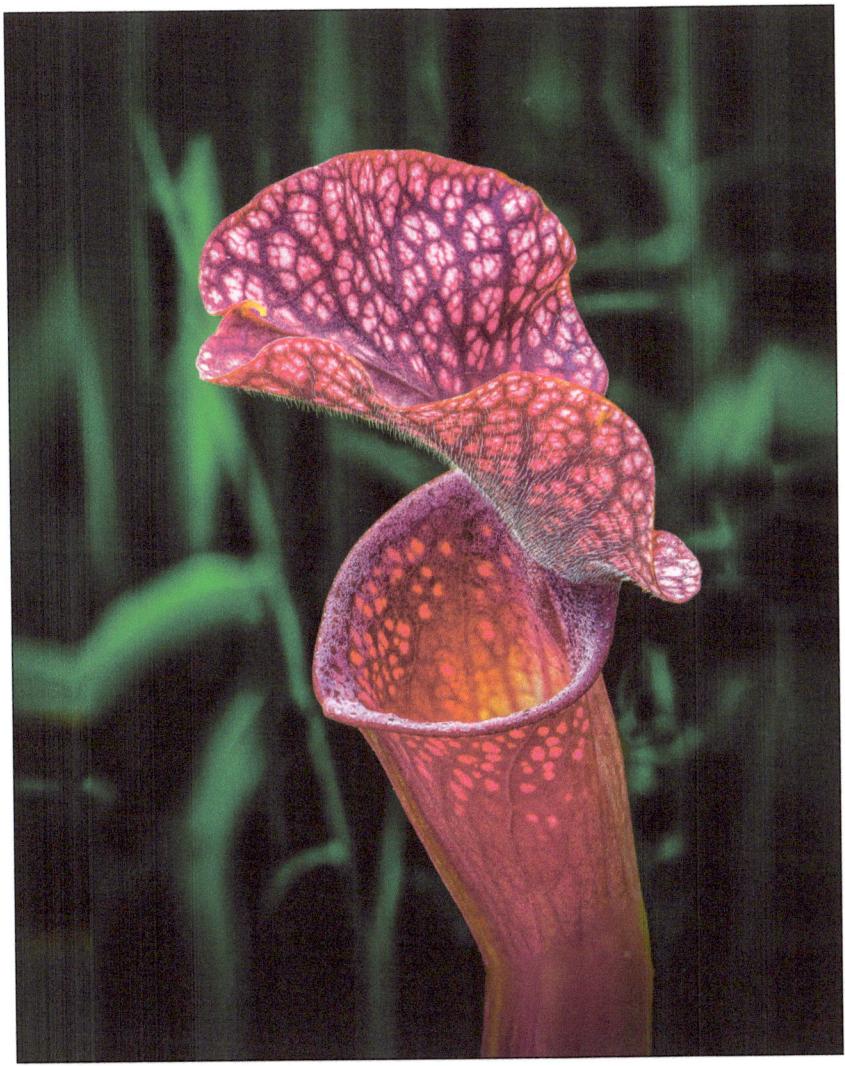

Let's Eat

Pitcher plants are several different carnivorous plants that have evolved modified leaves known as a pitfall traps – a prey-trapping mechanism featuring a deep cavity filled with liquid.

Nikon D90, 18-105 mm zoom, ISO (formerly ASA) 200, f/8 @ 1/5 sec. Processed with Adobe Lightroom and Photoshop

BENNETT, ROGER H., Buffalo, N.Y.
(Photography) Tau Epsilon Phi;
Photo Society; *Techmila*; Hillel

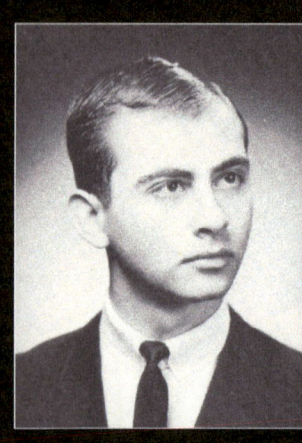

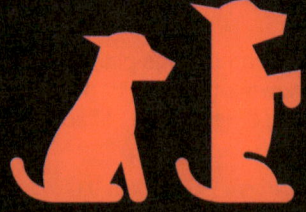

ROGER **BENNETT**

Bachelor of Fine Arts

Upon graduation Roger moved to California from Buffalo. He and his father opened a retail photography business in a suburb of Los Angeles. Roger credits his education at RIT with giving him the tools to be successful in the retail sector and as a photography teacher.

Roger, now retired, travels and shoots digital images. He is still active in teaching Photoshop classes.

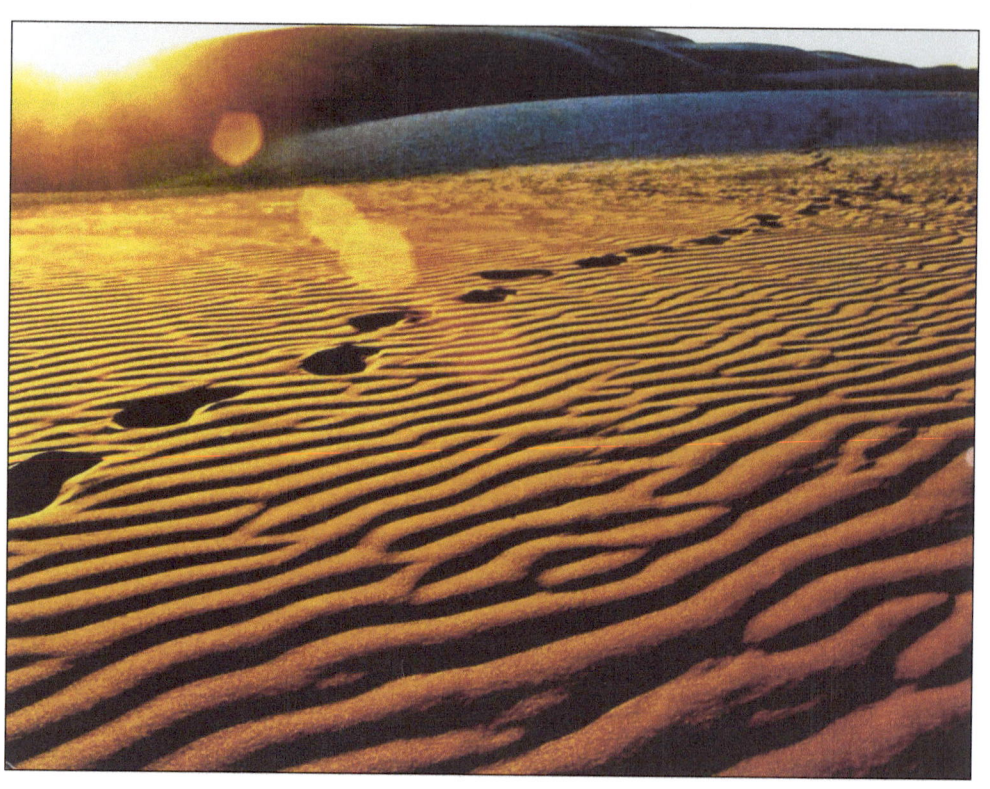

FILM

End of Watch, Seal Beach, CA

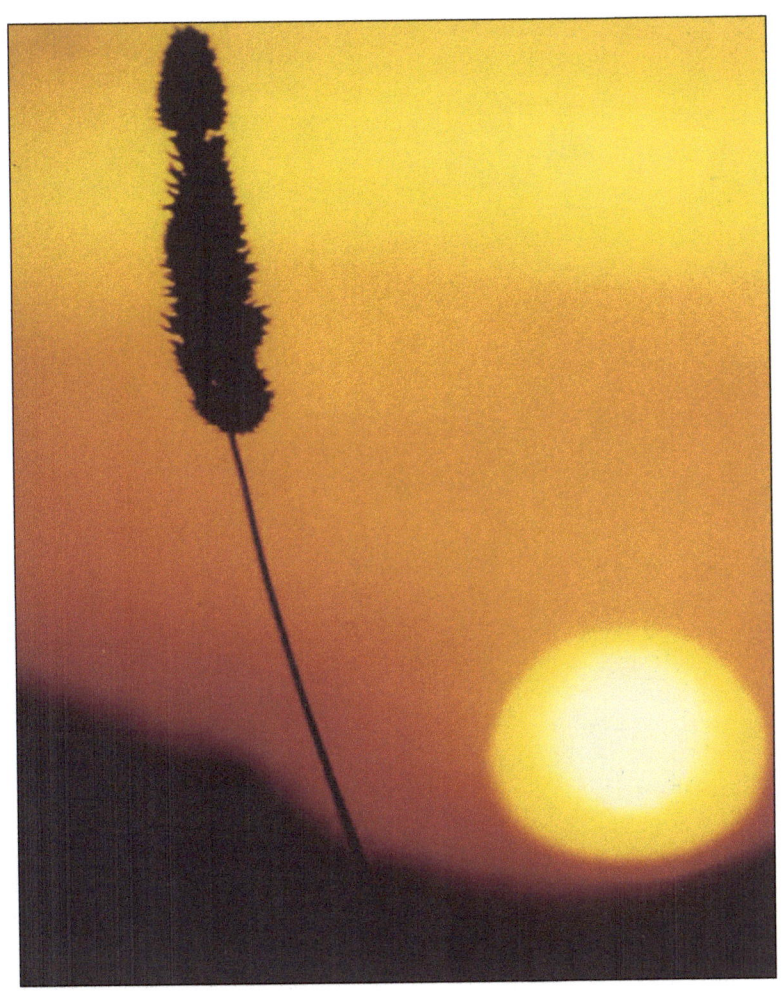

DIGITAL

First Impression, Pismo Beach, CA

COCHRAN, GEORGE M., North Bergen, N.J.
(Photography)

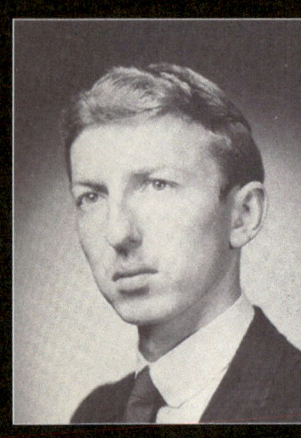

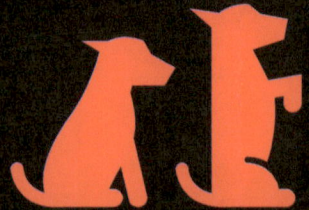

GEORGE **COCHRAN**

Bachelor of Fine Arts

From an assistant to several advertising studios in New York City, George has evolved into a successful career in advertising, marketing, and visual media in New York, Chicago, and Los Angeles. His work with agencies like J. Walter Thompson, Young & Rubicam, Saatchi & Saatchi and many others has won both acclaim and awards. Moving to Charlotte, NC 12 years ago he established Cochran Enterprises to consult with companies on communication strategies in print, TV, radio, and digital media.

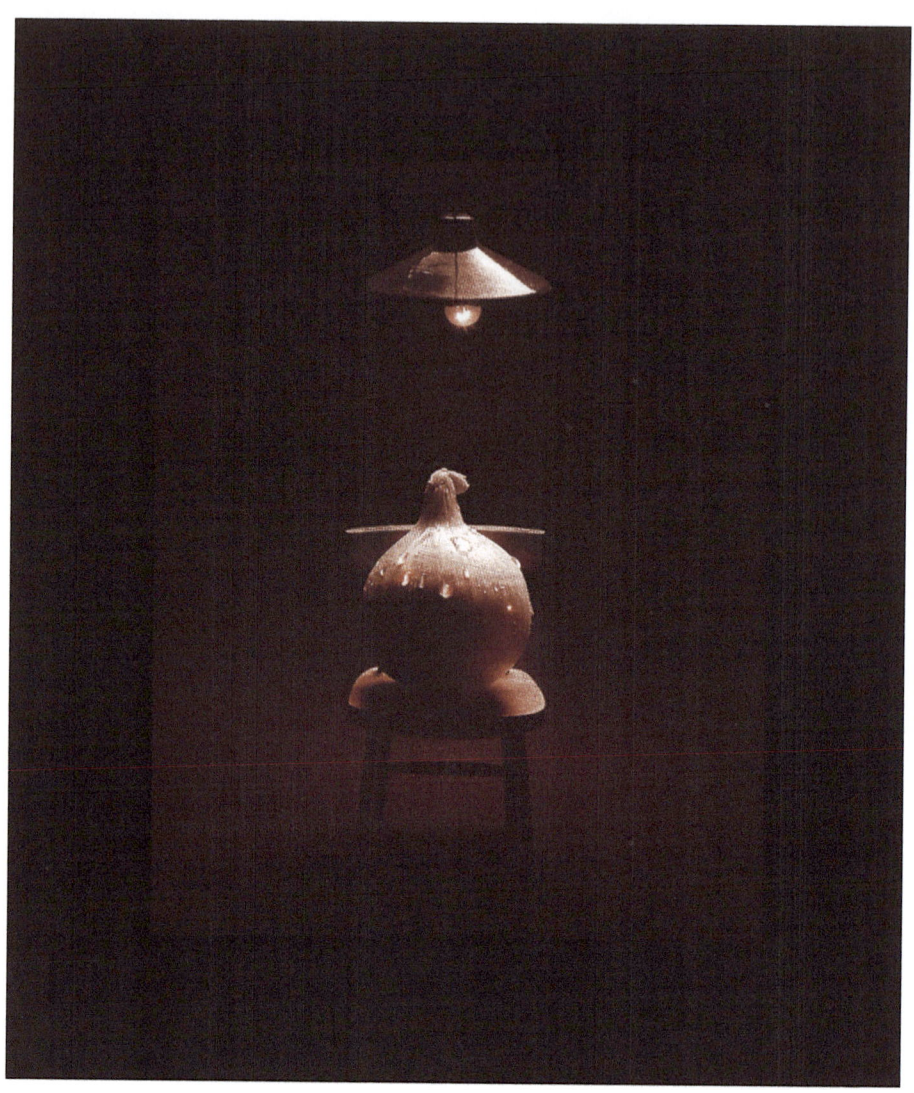

FILM

Grilled Onion

Advertising photograph for Eastman Kodak, 1969

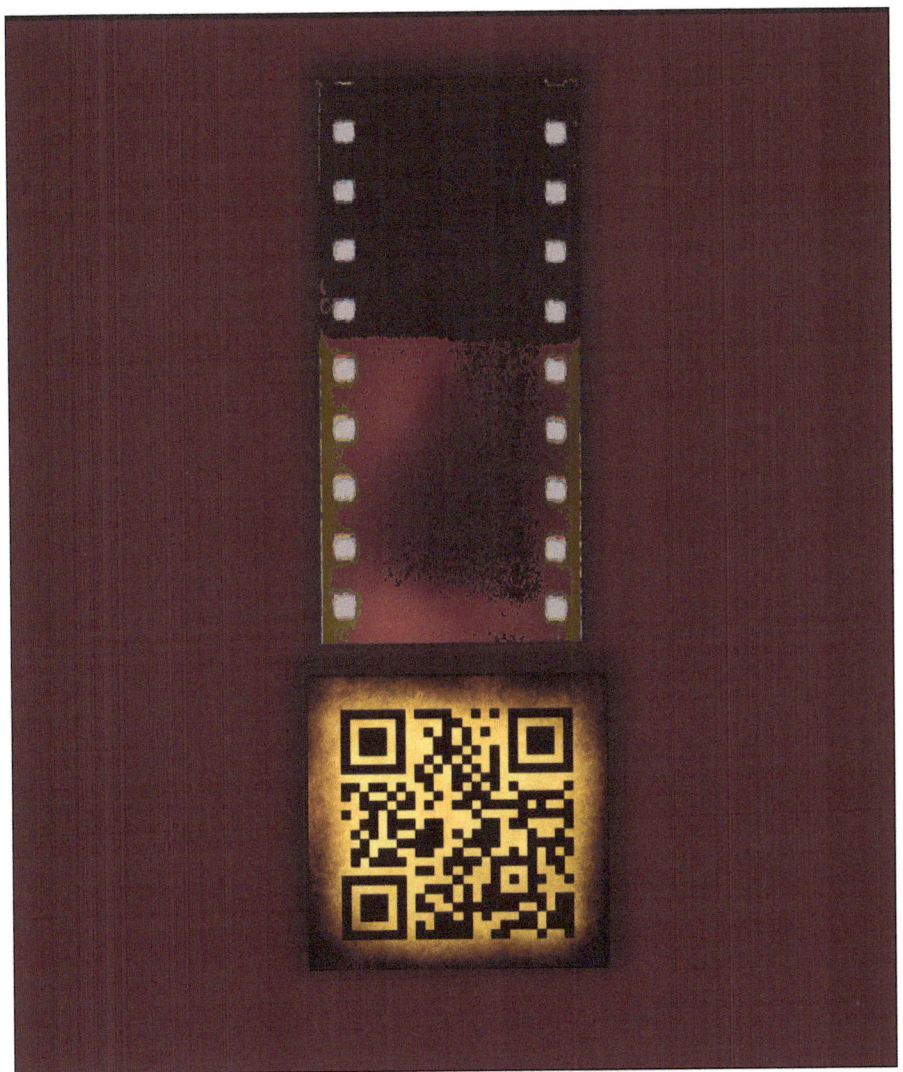

DIGITAL

QR Code

Scan the code and go on a digital journey

CORNELL, JOHN H., Glen Head, N.Y.
(Photography) Techmila, Reporter, Photo Society

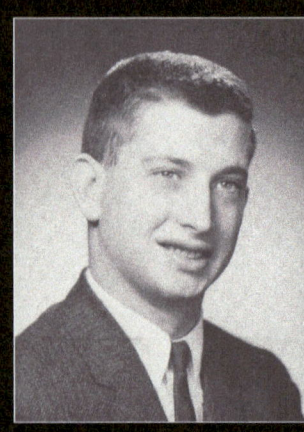

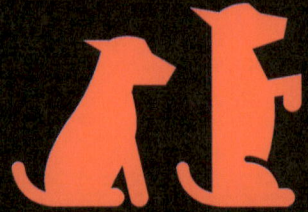

JOHN **CORNELL**

Bachelor of Fine Arts
Master of Business Administration, Adelphi University

Immediately following graduation from RIT John worked for two years at *Newsday* newspaper on Long Island, NY. He then became Director of Photography at International Nickel Company in New York City.

In 1972 he returned to his roots, home, and *Newsday* where he worked until 2003. The *Newsday* staff was cited in 1997 by the Pulitzer Committee for "its enterprising coverage of the crash of TWA Flight 800 and its aftermath."

During his time at the paper he won numerous awards, was President of the National Press Photographers Association, and co-founded the Electronic Photojournalism Workshop.

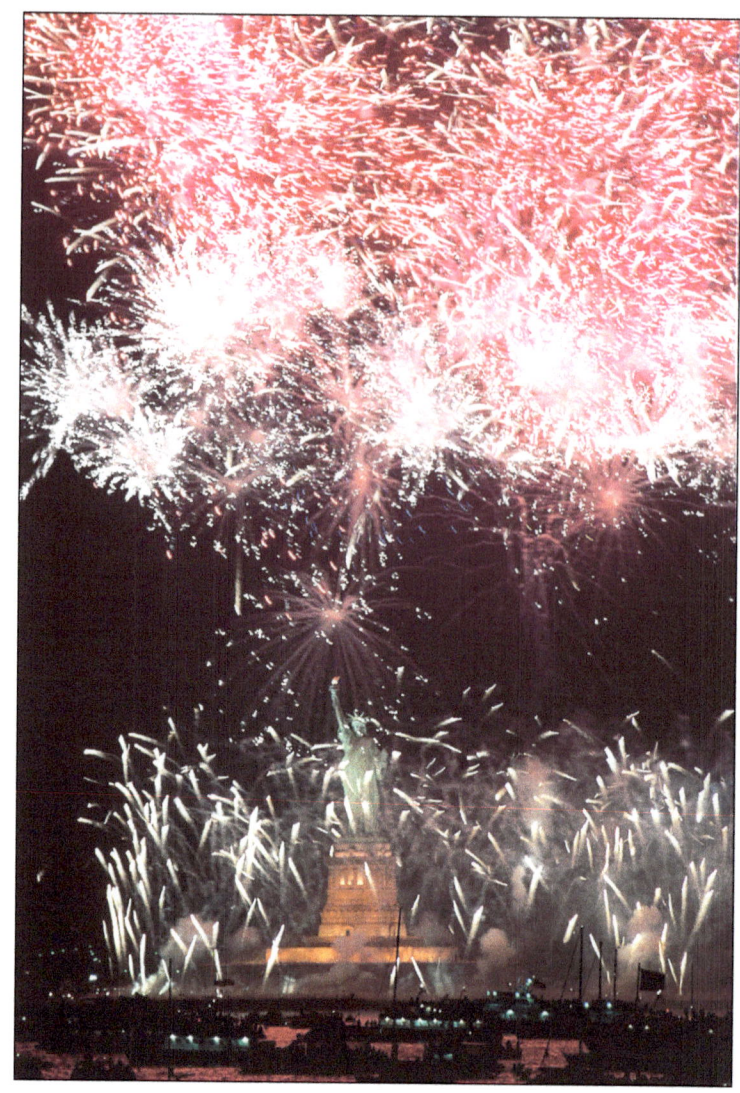

FILM

July 4, 1986 – New York Harbor, Red Hook, Brooklyn Warehouse Roof

The final minutes of the of the aerial fireworks display to celebrate the re-lighting of the Statue of Liberty torch in New York Harbor.

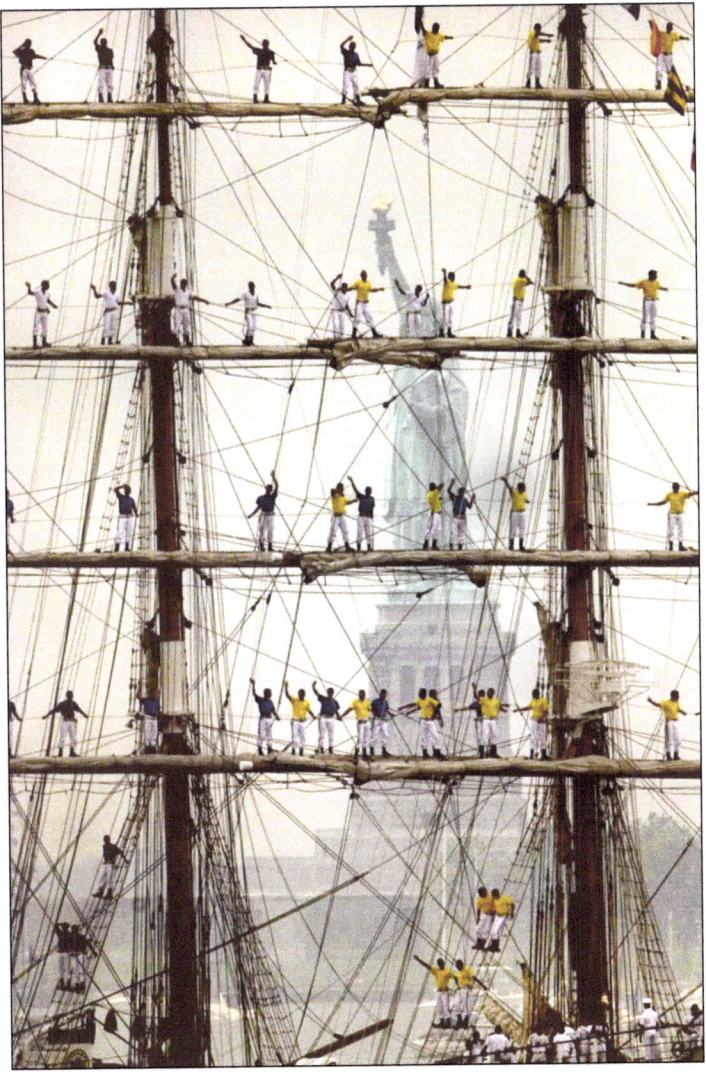

DIGITAL

July 4, 2000 – New York Harbor (The Battery)

The tall ship Simon Bolivar passes the Statue of Liberty during Op Sail 2000. Sailors on the rigging salute the City of New York.

After downloading the image to a laptop the file was sent to the paper via a cell phone connection.

ENGELDRUM, PETER G., Red Bank, N.J.
(Photography) SPSE; Photo Society

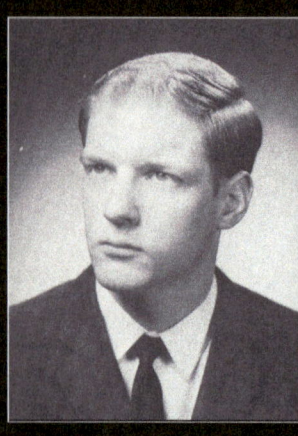

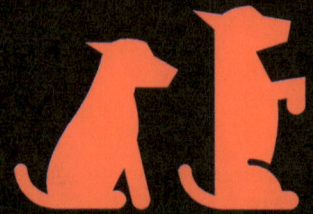

PETER **ENGELDRUM**

Bachelor of Science
Master of Science – RIT

During the eight years following his graduation Pete worked for the "military industrial complex" with Perkin-Elmer and CBS. He returned to RIT for his Master of Science in Photographic Science. Xerox offered him the opportunity with a "golden handshake" to form his company, Imcotek. For the next 25 years he worked with a long list of imaging companies by providing expertise in imaging and color science.

Pete has been awarded 12 patents, published numerous technical articles, and wrote and published the *Psychometric Scaling* book. Awards, lectures, and thesis advising have been a large part of his continued relationship with RIT in Imaging Science and the Munsell Color Science program.

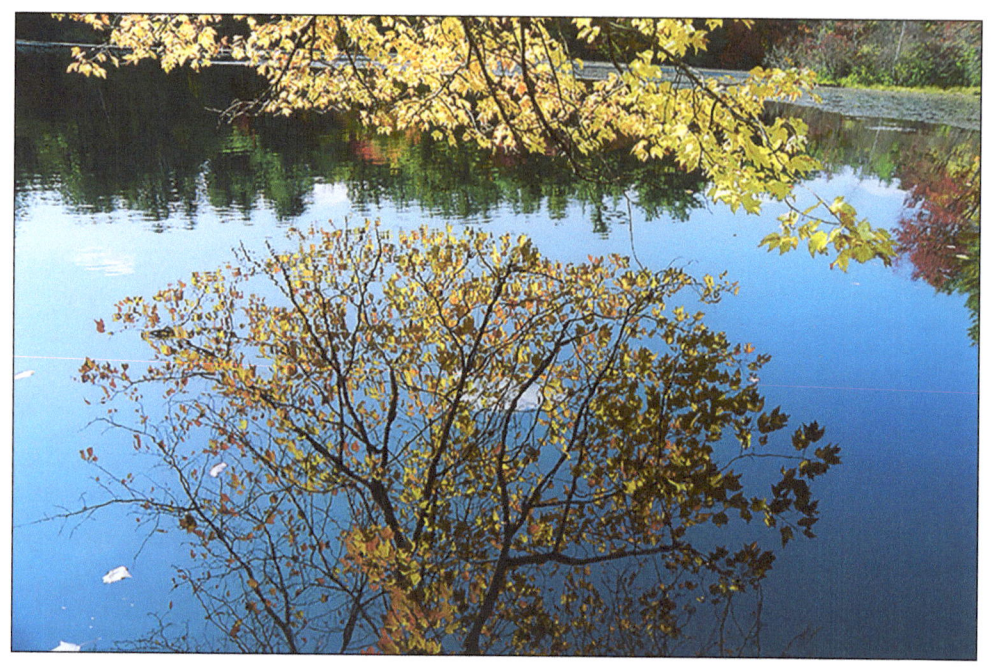

FILM

October, 2004 – Fall on Hutchins Pond Massachusetts

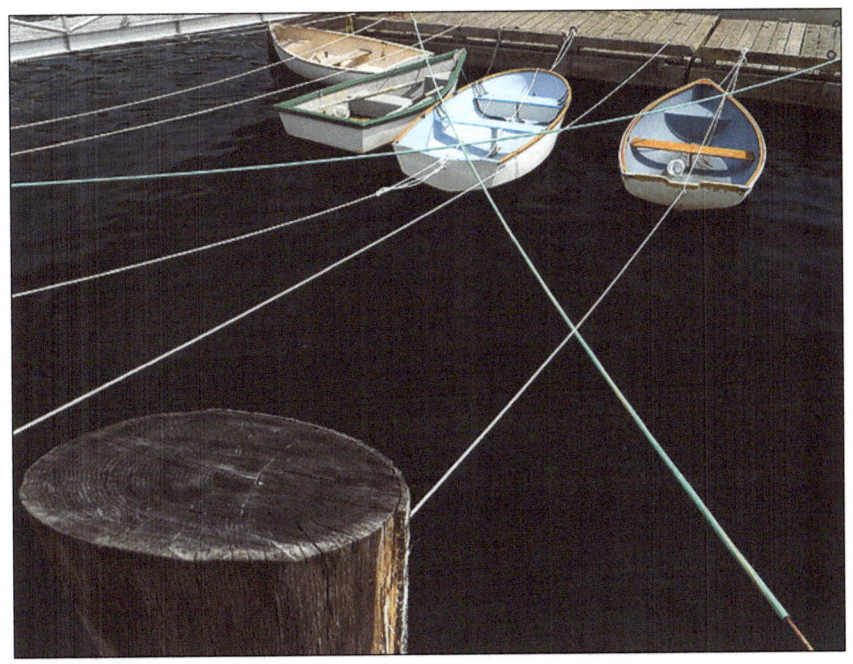

DIGITAL

July, 2005 – Ties That Bind

Olympus C 8080WZ; ISO (ASA) 50, f/7.1 @ 1/60 sec.

GEISSINGER, MICHAEL A., Huntingdon, PA.
(Photography) Fencing;
Ski Club; Letterman's Club

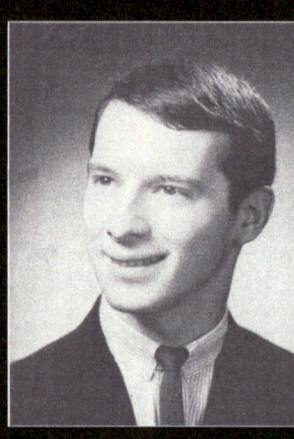

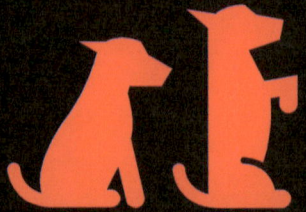

MICHAEL **GEISSINGER**

Bachelor of Fine Arts
Master of Science-RIT

Through a temporary Air Force assignment Mike landed at the White House as a staff photographer during the administration of President Lyndon Johnson. As part of a team of four photographers, working under chief photographer Yoichi R. Okamoto, he was charged with documenting the administration for history. Unprecedented access to meetings and events during this tumultuous time enabled the group to create a body of work which still stands as a pillar in presidential documentary photography.

After leaving the White House on January 20, 1969, Mike became the Director of Photography at Virginia Polytechnic Institute and State University (VA Tech). In 1971 he returned to his Alma Mater to teach photojournalism. Mike took part in a faculty exchange program with Shanghai University of Technology in 1985. He spent 10 weeks in China teaching, traveling and shooting over 300 rolls of film.

"Getting the bug" to shoot he, and his wife Barbara, moved to Washington, DC in 1986 where he had a successful freelance photography business. Clients included the *New York Times*, *Los Angeles Times*, *Newsday*, as well as corporations and associations. Mike is a past president of the White House News Photographers' Association.

Mike is an accomplished sailor and has made two trans-Atlantic voyages.

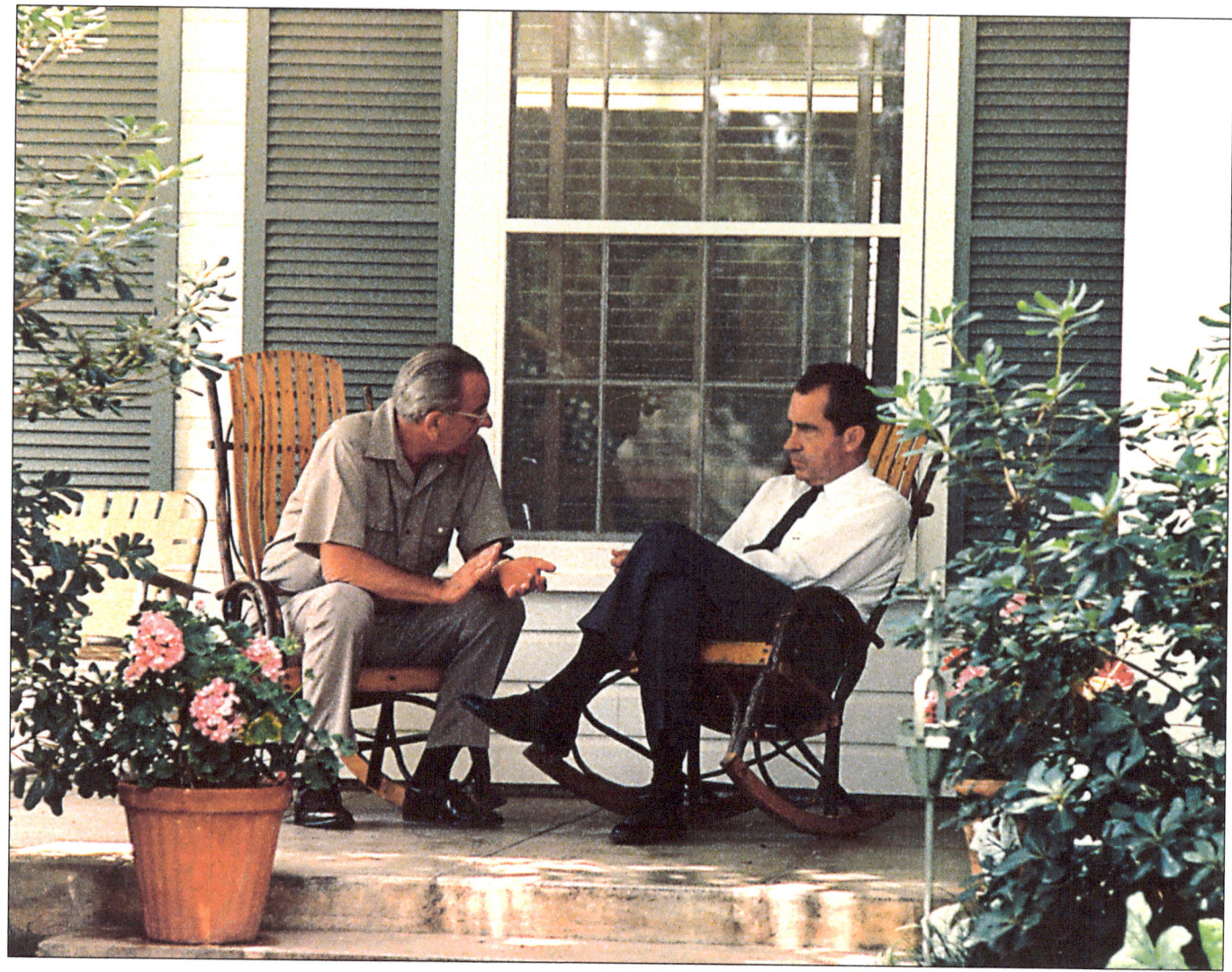

FILM

LBJ & RMN – August 10, 1968

After receiving the presidential nomination of the
Republican Party in 1968, Richard Nixon stopped at
the Texas Ranch to meet with President Johnson.
They sat on the porch for private discussions.

*Nikon F with a 200mm f/4 lens, Kodacolor X negative color
film at ASA (ISO) 80.*

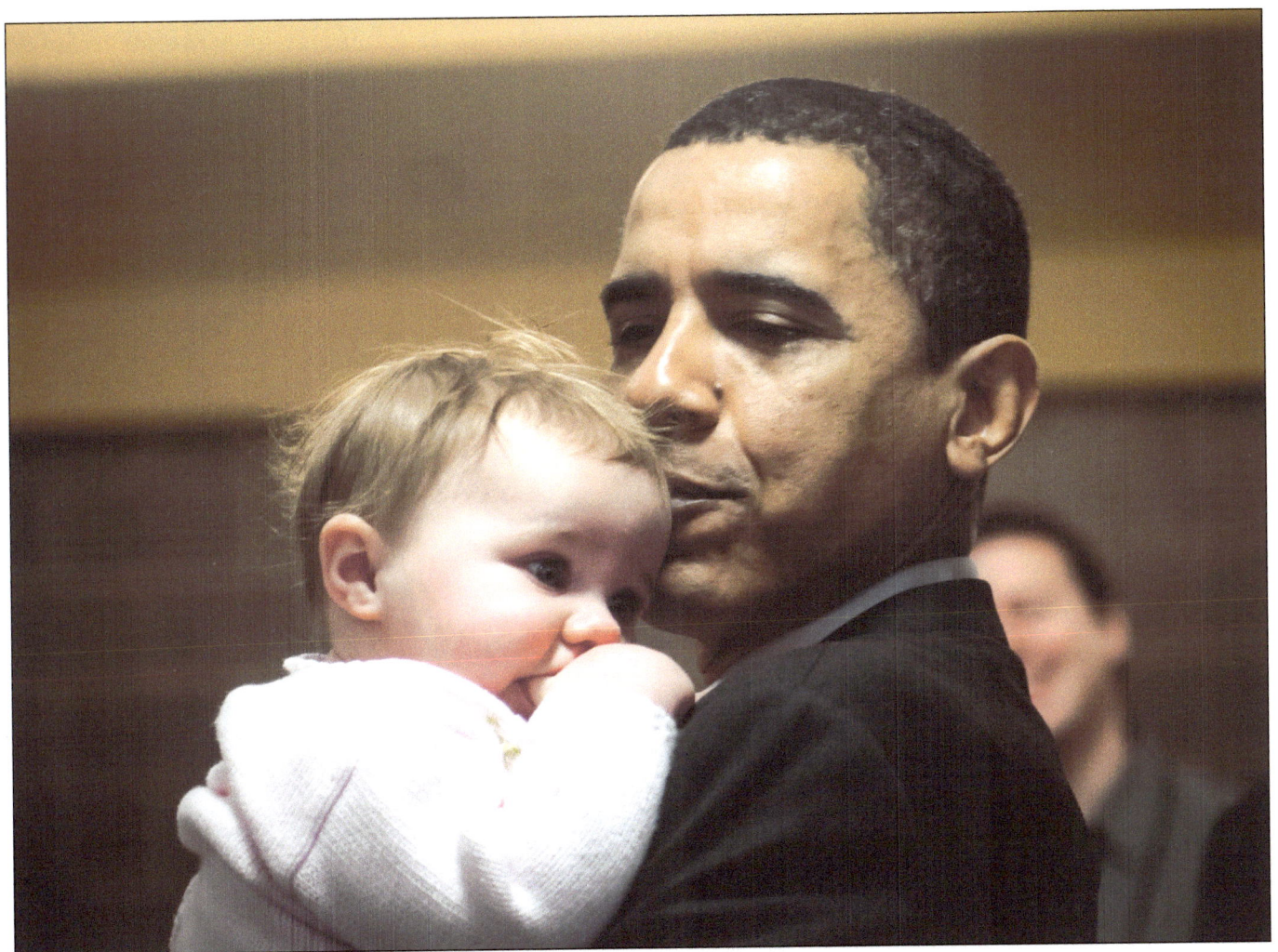

DIGITAL

Barack Obama & Baby – February 10, 2008

Candidate Obama made a campaign stop in Alexandria, VA
to hold a rally and town hall meeting. Following the town hall
a proud father handed his baby to Obama and, like all
good politicians, he kissed the baby.

Nikon D70, f/2.8 @ 1/60 sec, ISO (ASA) 640

GILSON, KEVIN R., Marcellus, N.Y.
(Photography) Newman Club; Choraliers; WITR

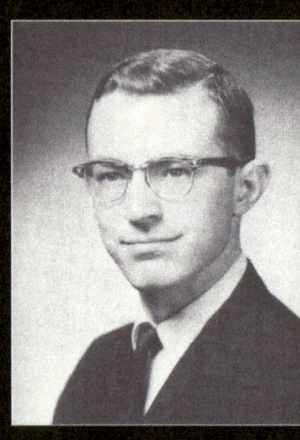

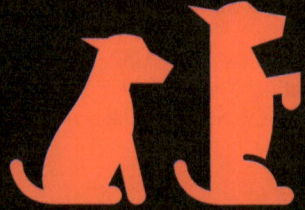

KEVIN **GILSON**

Bachelor of Science
Master of Science-University of Dayton

Kevin has spent his career in quality management systems in the aerospace and healthcare industries. Working with the leading companies, in the 70's and 80's, he was involved with NASA and Goddard Space Flight Center testing and evaluating imaging systems, hardware and software. Kevin has over 10 years of experience in photographic systems and digital satellite image reconstruction. He has a proven background in international standards implementation, auditing, and quality systems training programs.

In his free time, Kevin enjoys performing early music, model railroading, bicycling and walking.

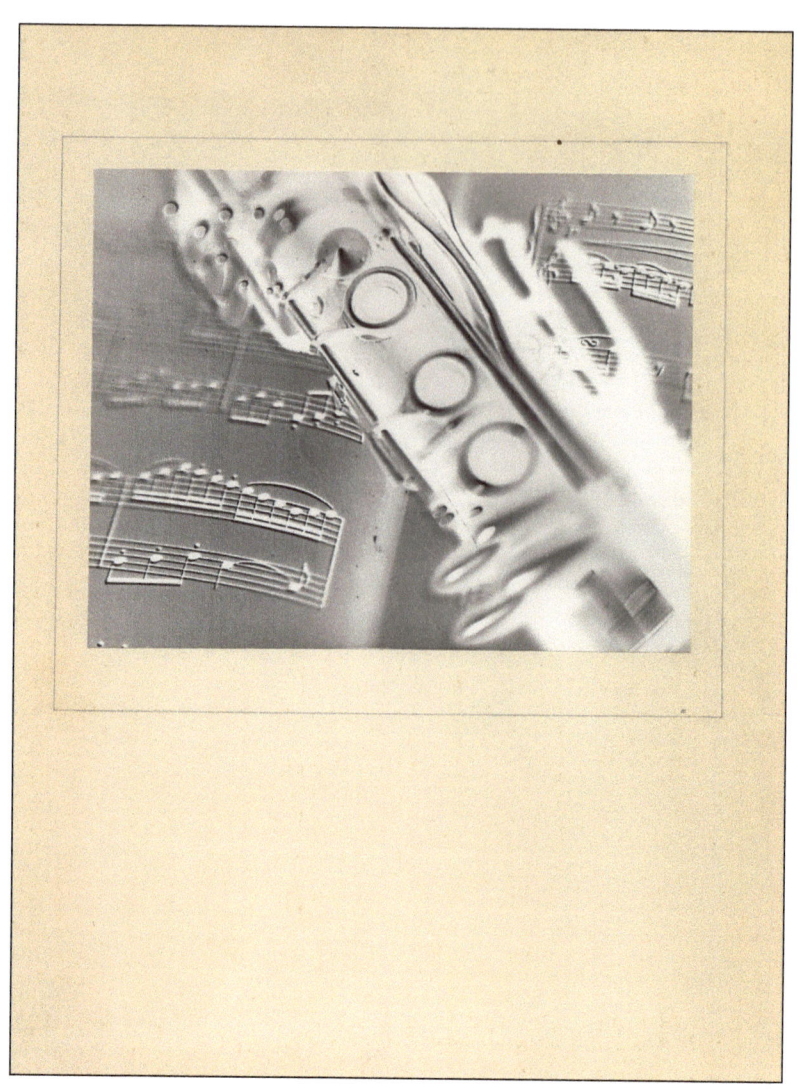

FILM

Untitled

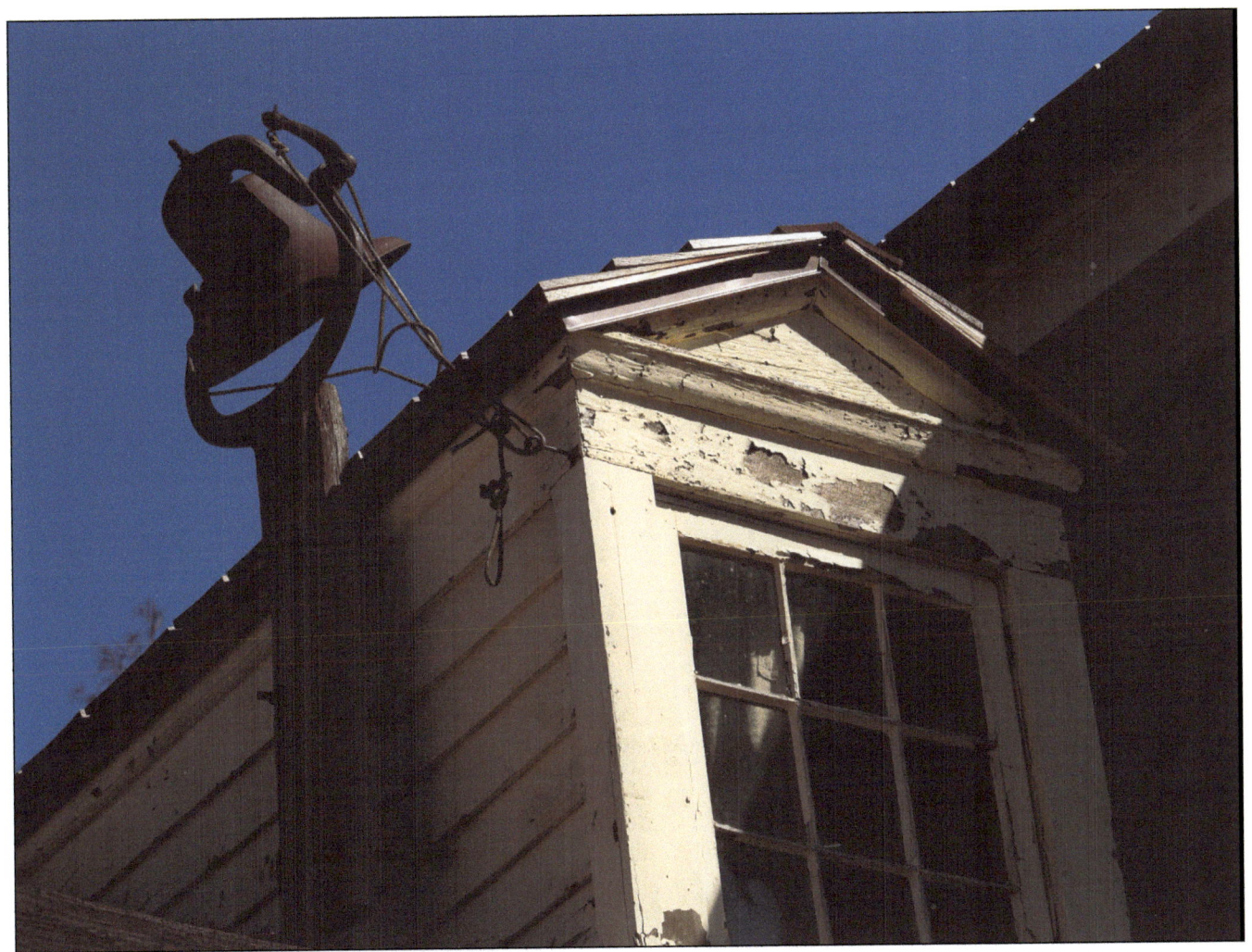

DIGITAL

Untitled

KINNEY, WILLIAM C., Norwich, Conn.
(Photography) Delta Lamda Epsilon

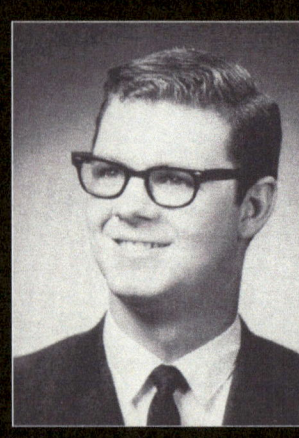

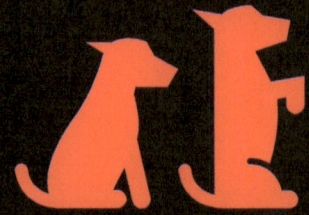

BILL **KINNEY**

Bachelor of Science

After graduation Bill made his home in California. He worked for Houston Fearless on aerospace image processing and Technicolor in color TV and movies. and at ITEK on satellite and space imaging. He and a partner started MICROTECK, imaging systems for x-ray microfilming. With his wife Molly, he started GRAYSCALE Labs where he holds several patents for medical x-ray microfilming equipment.

Bill had his fill of corporate life. He spent six years building a 43' sailboat called *Sanctuary* which launched in 1982. Bill and Molly spent the next ten-years cruising the US East Coast, Caribbean and Mediterranean. Back on dry land, Bill now spends his time producing photo paintings.

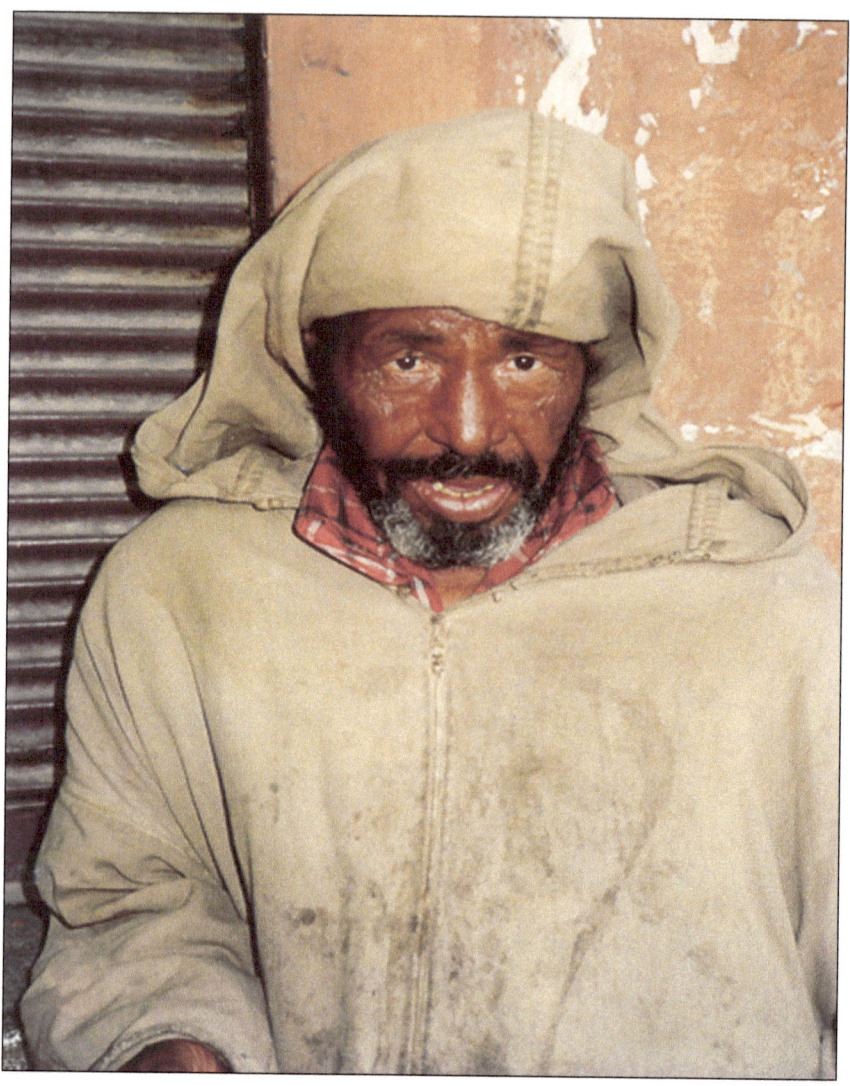

FILM

The Face of Morocco

Traditional 35mm camera with color negative film

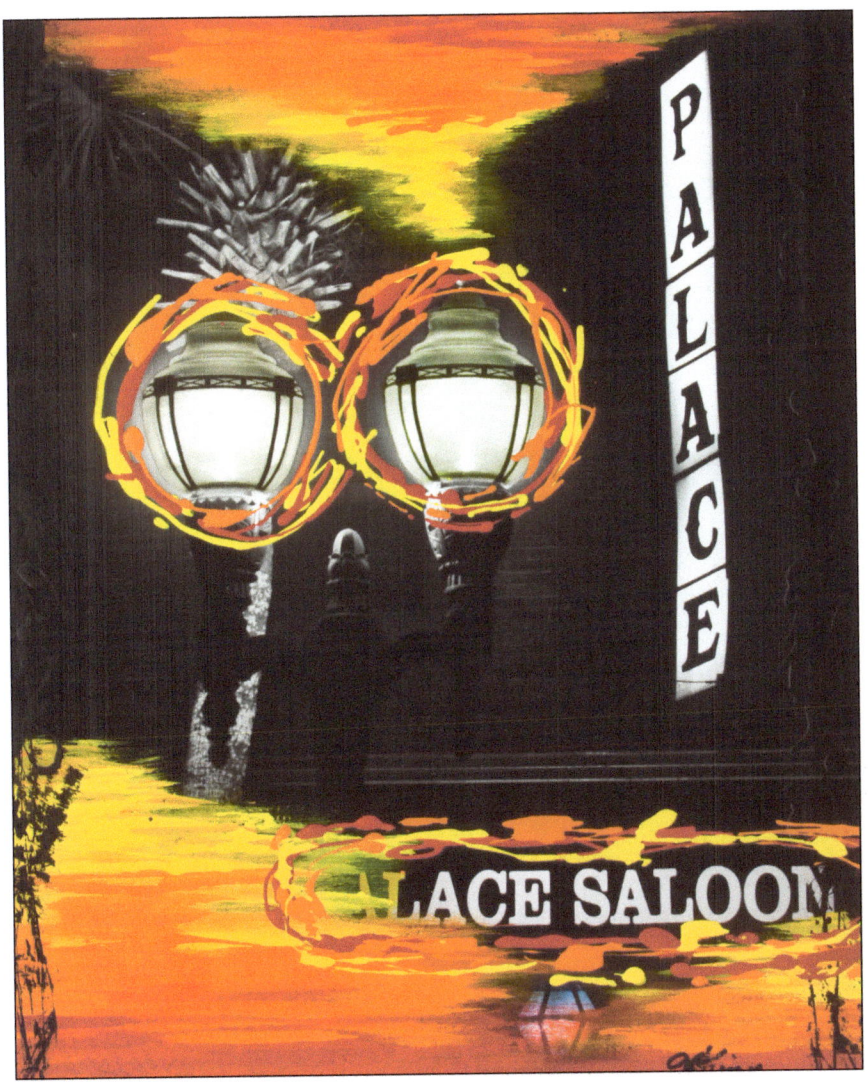

DIGITAL

Florida's Oldest Saloon

Conventional digital image converted to black & white with acrylic paint applied with a brush or knife.

LANGONE, JAMES A., Wilbraham, Mass.
(Photography) SPSE; Ski Club;
Delta Lambda Epsilon

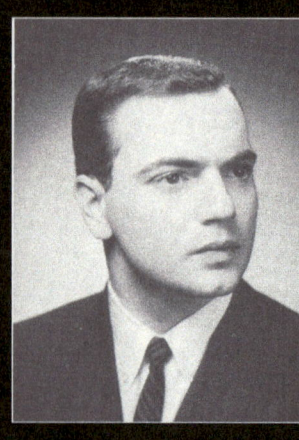

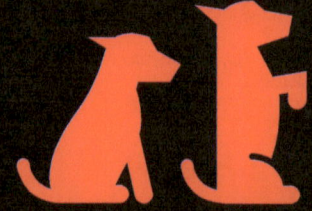

JAMES **LANGONE**

Bachelor of Science
Master of Science - RIT

Jim currently runs a commercial photographic illustration studio in Springfield, MA. With national and international clients he, and his five full time photographers, use both conventional film and digital technologies to produce award-winning images.

Professor Langone teaches at Springfield Technical Community College and is a technical consultant in photography and digital imaging. A scuba diver for over 30 years his images have been exhibited and published throughout the world.

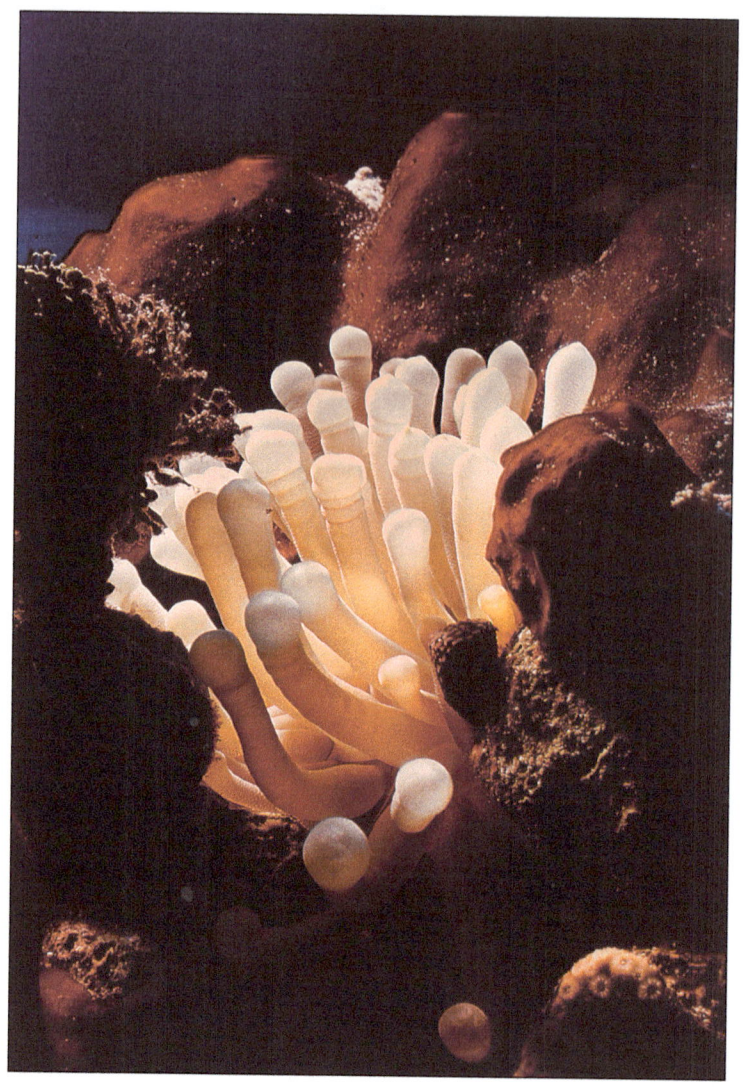

FILM

Anemone I

Sea anemones are a group of water-dwelling, predatory animals of the order Actiniaria.

Nikonos 35mm underwater camera with Kodak VPS negative color film

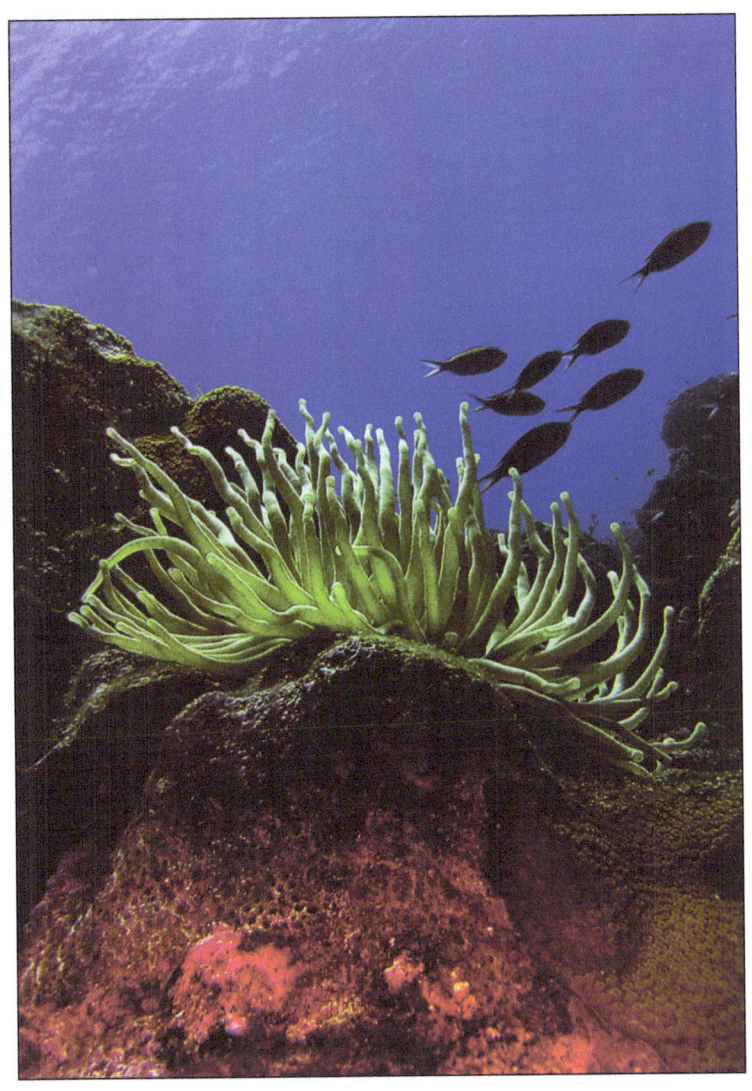

DIGITAL

Anemone II

Sea and Sea DX 8000G camera on Secure Digital card

LEWIS, JEROME J., Pampa, Texas
(Photography) Sigma Pi; Fencing;
Student Council; Newman Cub

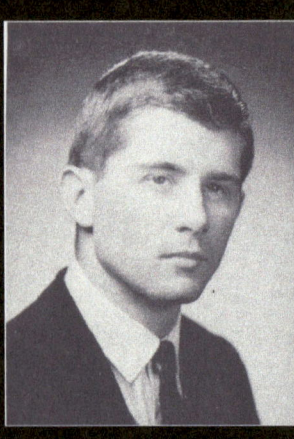

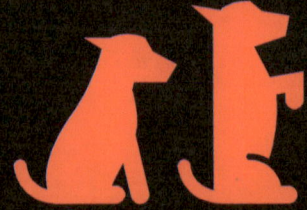

JERRY **LEWIS**

Bachelor of Fine Arts

Carhart Photo, Inc. was a large, regional photo finishing company with offices in Rochester. Following graduation Jerry went to work for the company and, rising through the ranks, retired as President in 1980. He then started a retail hair care operation and is the creator of *Sport Clips Haircuts* franchise. Jerry develops and manages commercial real estate.

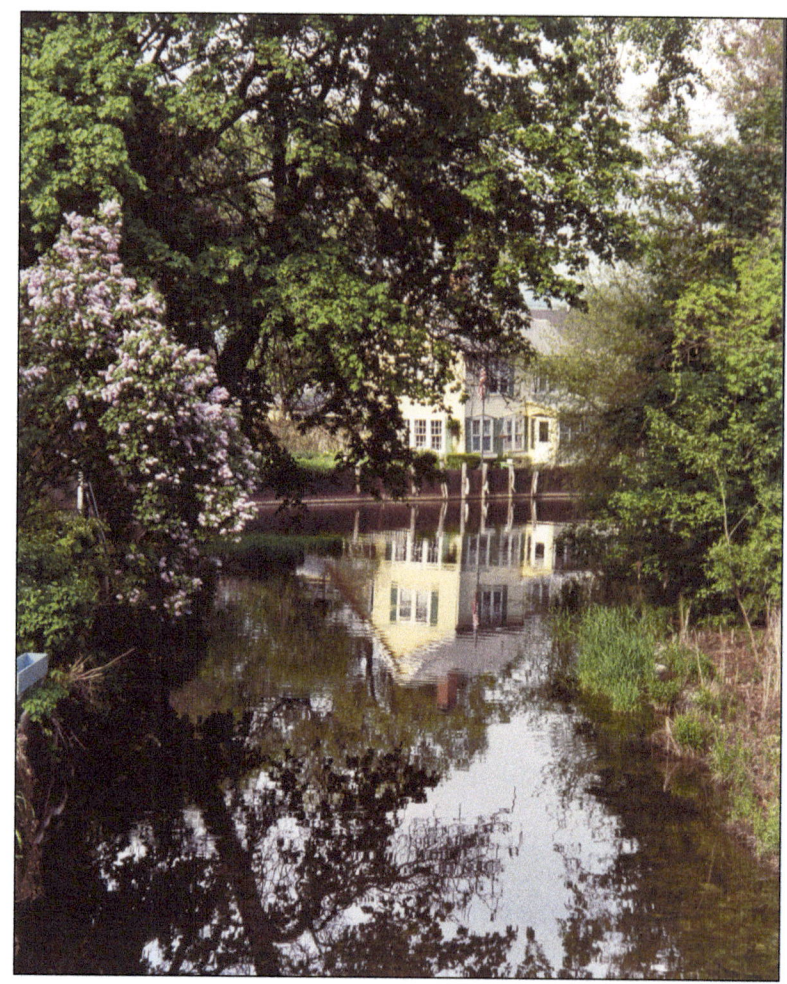

FILM

Untitled

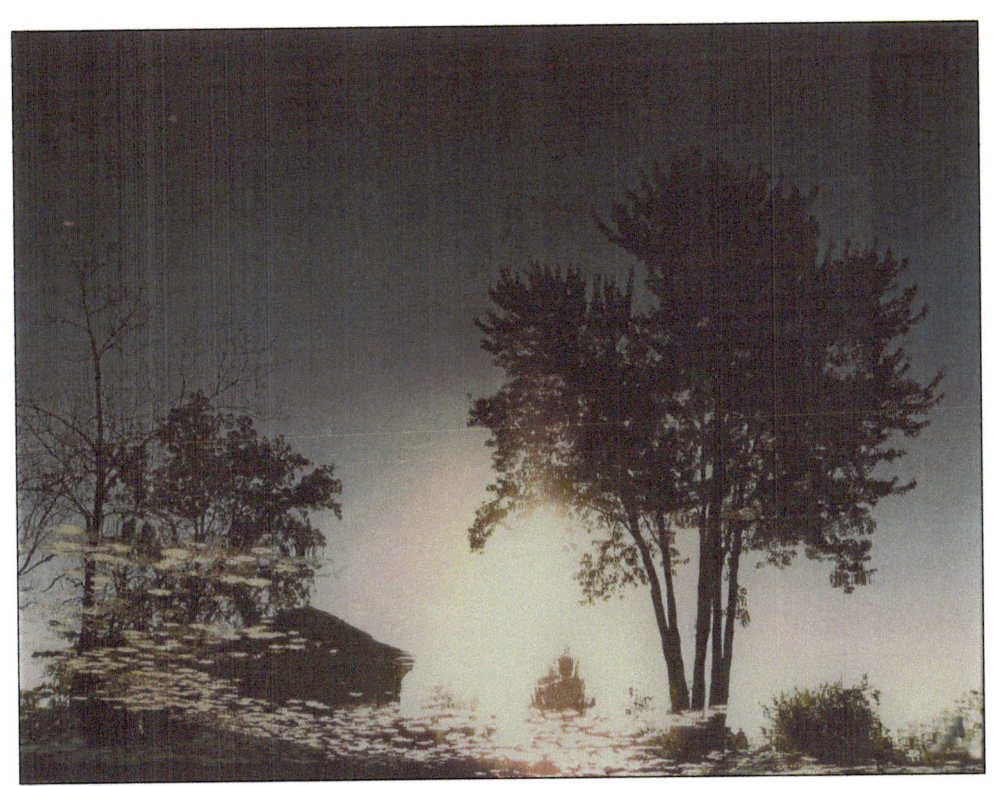

DIGITAL

Untitled

SHERMAN, RON A., University Hgts., Ohio *(Photography)* Tau Epsilon Phi; Hillel; Student Council, President

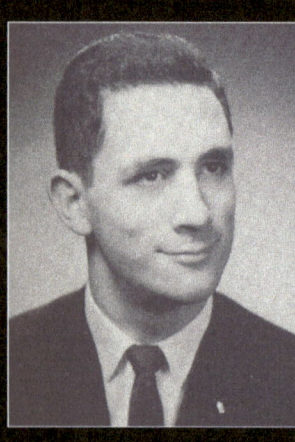

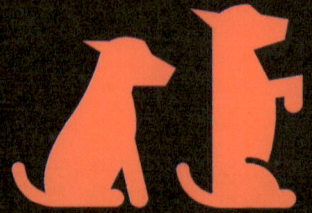

RON **SHERMAN**

Bachelor of Fine Arts

Ron is based in Atlanta, GA running an advertising, corporate, and editorial photography operation. His clients include national and international publications and corporations. Ron has produced marketing and publication photography for over 125 colleges and universities throughout the U.S. and Canada. Four books on Atlanta have featured his photographs and he runs a company that combines photography and computer technology.

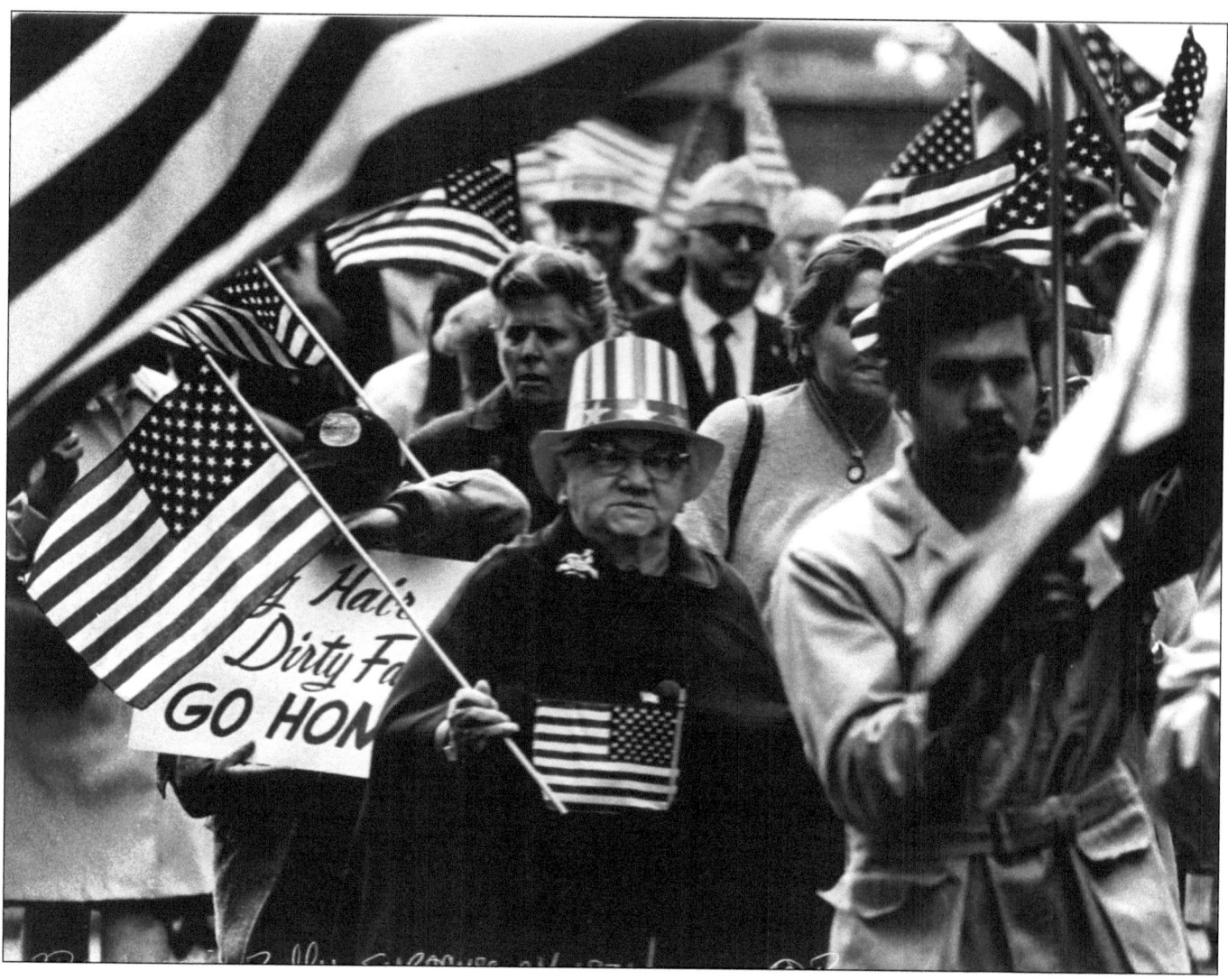

FILM

1971 – Pro-America Rally, Syracuse, NY

Several hundred people marched in Syracuse, NY to challenge the protesters of the Viet Nam War.

This image was published in *Life* magazine's 1972 *Pictures of the Year* edition.

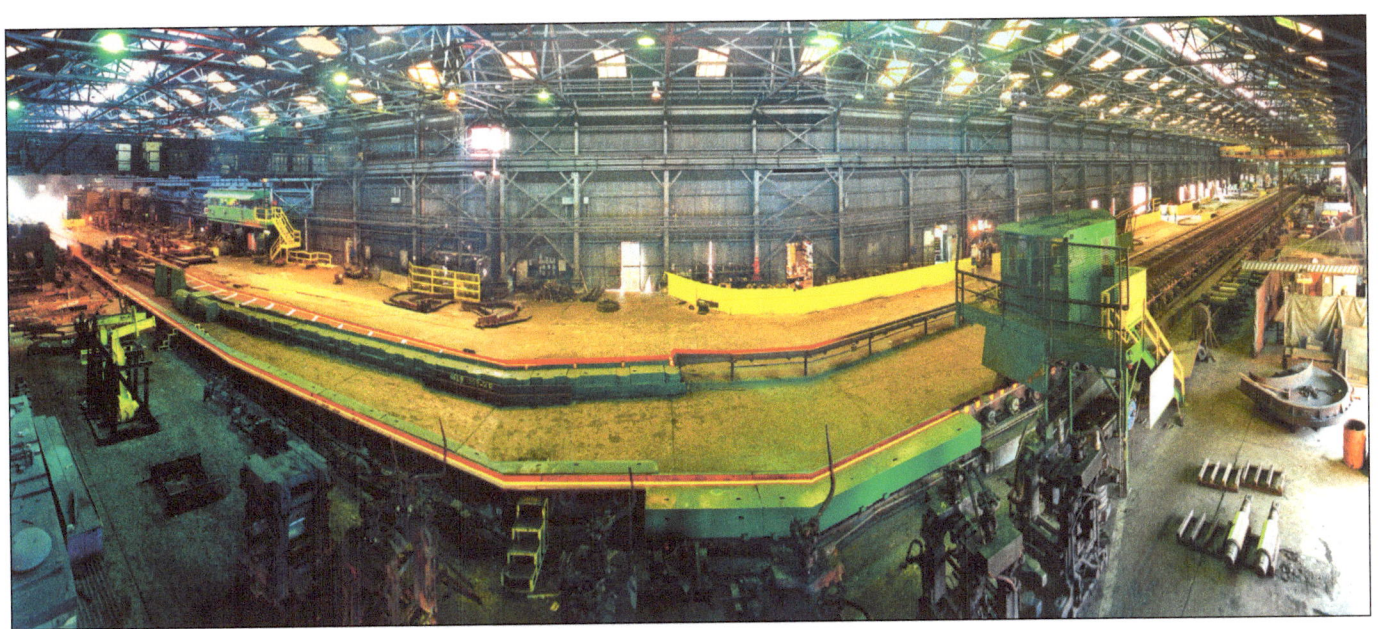

DIGITAL'

Atlantic Steel 13 Inch Roll Bar in the 740 Foot Facility

*The final image combined 7 individual images into a panorama
for a 19.5" wide three-fold brochure,*

SPENCER, KENNETH C., Milford, Conn.
(Photography) Delta Lamda Epsilon;
Reporter, Fencing

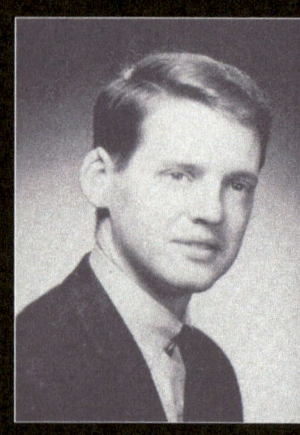

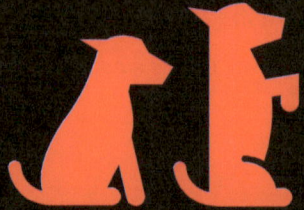

KEN **SPENCER**

Bachelor of Fine Arts

Following a two and one half year stint at the Gannett Rochester Newspapers as a staff photographer, Ken was hired by the Long Island newspaper *Newsday* in 1966. Starting as a general assignment photographer, covering news, professional sports teams, and feature photography, Ken spent the next 41 years at the newspaper. In 1971 Ken moved to the new *Newsday Sunday Magazine* shooting features, food, fashion, architecture, gardens, sports, portraits, personalities, picture stories and photo essays. When the Sunday magazine folded in 1990, he worked for the feature section of the newspaper until 2008. Additionally Ken freelanced for Parent's Magazine.

As a licensed private pilot Ken became involved in low altitude aerial photography.

Ken lives in Sea Cliff, NY with his wife Katherine where they raised two daughters. As an amateur astronomer he builds telescopes including grinding and polishing his mirrors. His blog, *A Picture Each Day,* has been going since February, 2007, where Ken posts a photograph each day.

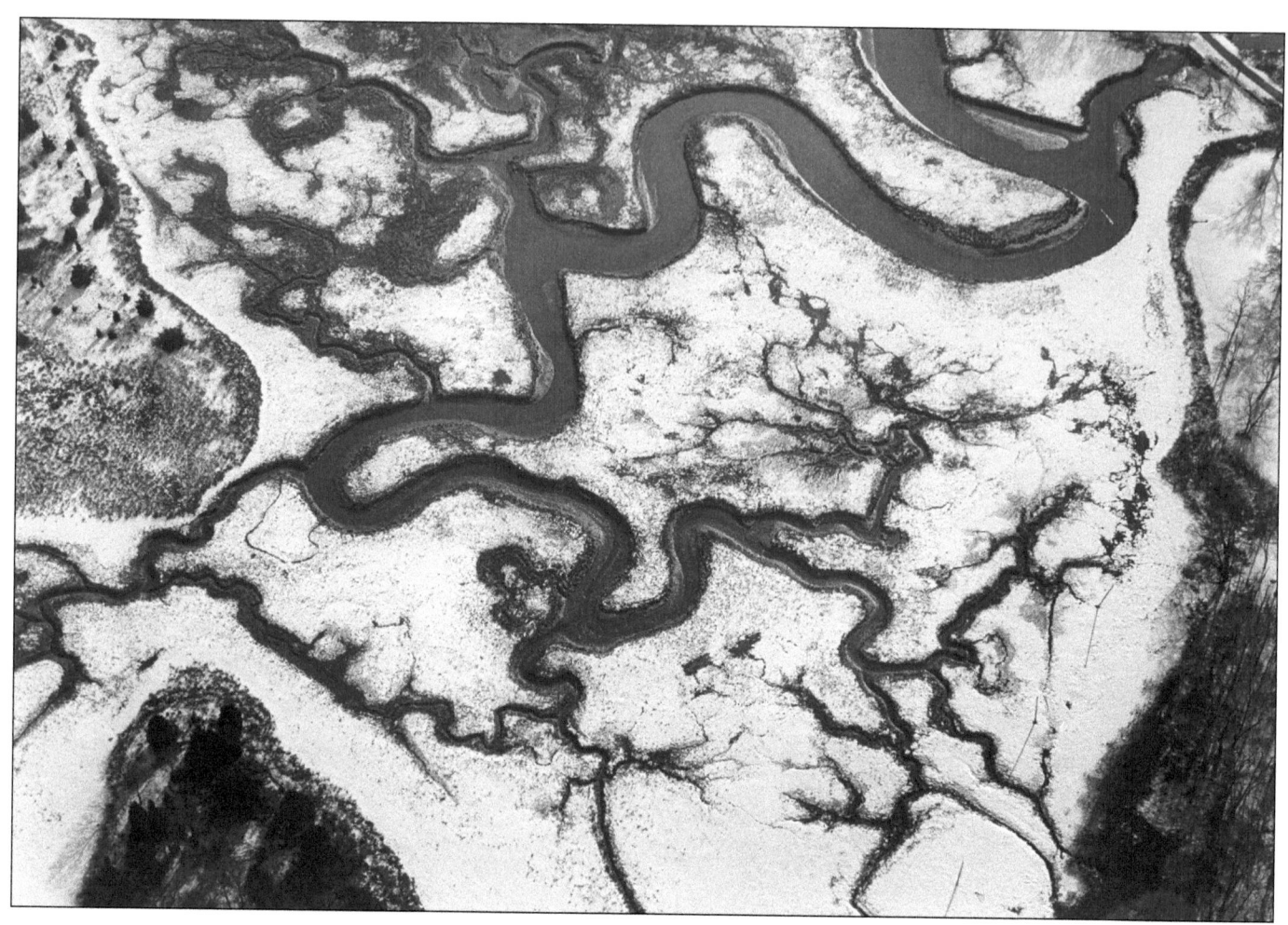

FILM

Meandering Stream, Centre Island, NY, 1984

This aerial photograph is a film image shot with a Nikon F3 camera and ISO 400 Kodak negative color film. When a subject did not require complex lighting setups, or long exposures, film was easy.

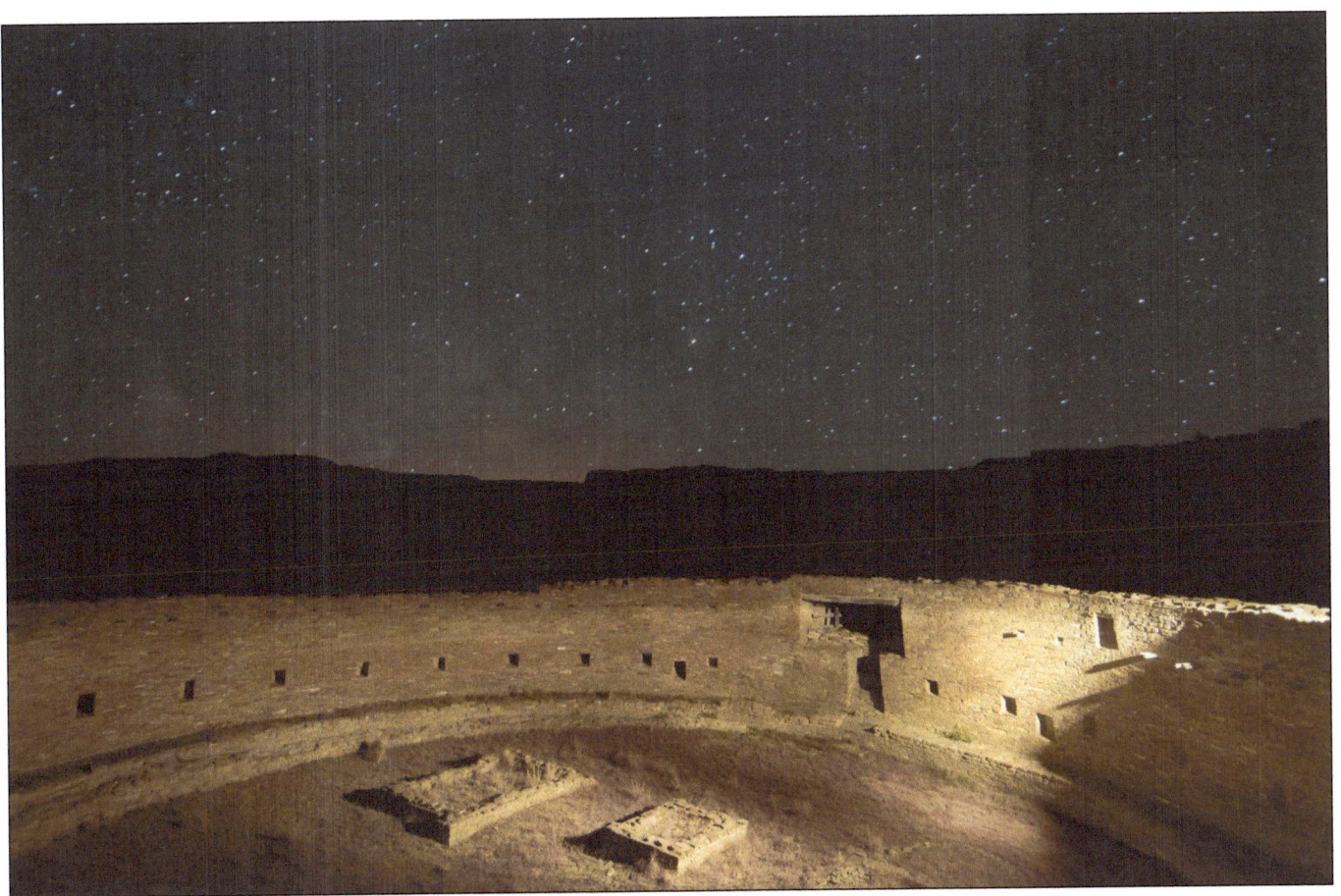

DIGITAL

**Great Kiva, Casa Rinconada,
Chaco Culture National Historical Park, AZ, 2011**

*This is a digital image made with a Nikon D-300 camera, ISO 3200,
1 minute exposure at f/4. The tricky technical part was balancing
the exposure for the sky and stars, with the exposure of the kiva
illuminated by the sweep of a flashlight.*

SPINDEL, DAVID M., Brooklyn, N.Y.
(Photography) Techmila, Photo Editor;
Hillel; Photo Society, President

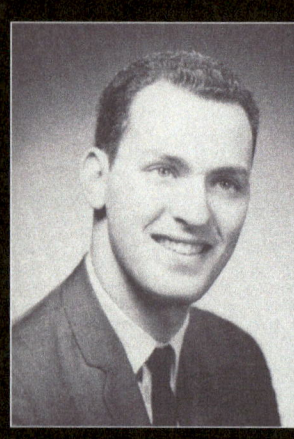

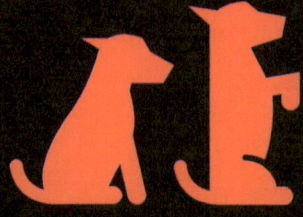

DAVID **SPINDEL**

Bachelor of Fine Arts

As a native New Yorker, Flatbush in Brooklyn, David only ventured out to attend RIT. He returned to "the city" and six years after graduation opened his own commercial advertising studio. He produced photographs for the advertising campaigns of national and international clients.

In the late 1970's he began doing photographic work for Major League Baseball and the New York Yankees. This led him to begin his collection of baseball memorabilia photography. John Lennon and Yoko Ono enlisted his services to photograph their *Double Fantasy* recording sessions. The results have been seen in books and documentaries of Lennon. Currently David and his wife Barbara live in Arizona.

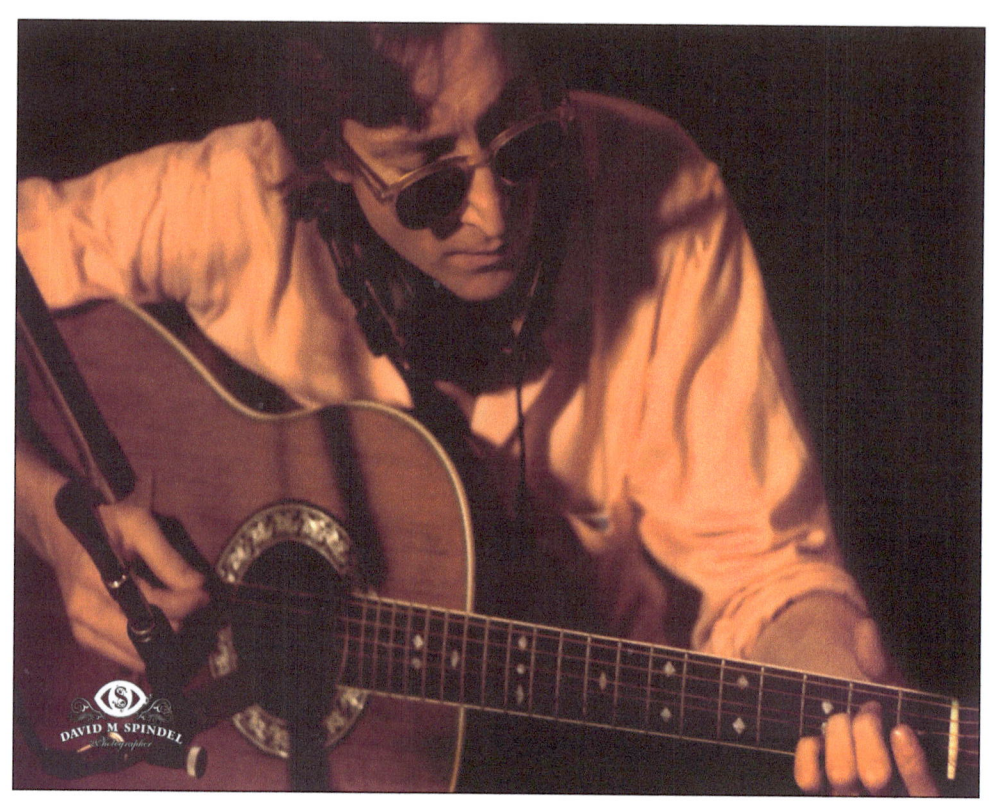

FILM

1980 – John Lennon

Photographed during the recording session
of the *Double Fantasy* album

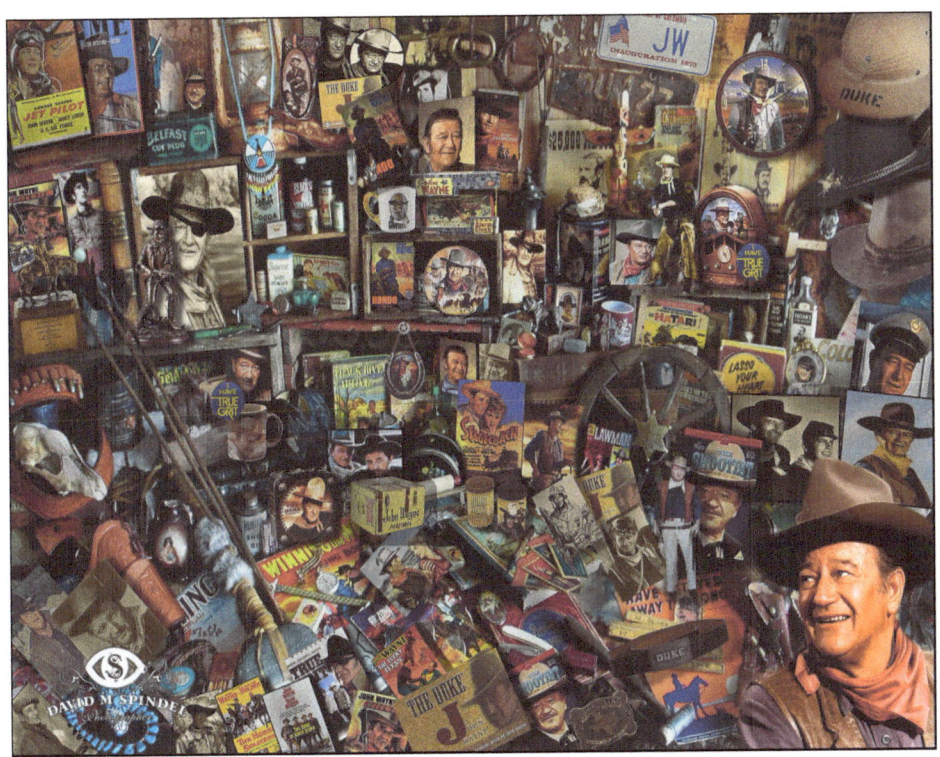

DIGITAL

2010 – John Wayne Collage

A collage representing the career of John Wayne.
Wayne's son provided the memorabilia.

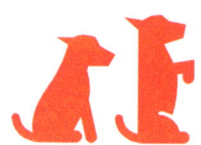

Book Design
BARBARA **BRECHER**

Bachelor of Fine Arts UMASS, Amherst/1972
Master of Fine Arts RIT, Communication Design/1974

Full disclosure: Barb has been married to Michael Geissinger (PH'64) for 35 years. They met at RIT while she was a graduate student in the Communication Design Department.

In 1986, after Barb and Mike moved to the Washington DC area, she established an award winning graphic design studio in Old Town Alexandria, VA. Her clients included the National Geographic Society, the American Red Cross, the National Park Service and other national and local corporations, museums, not- for-profit groups and associations. Currently Barb is the Executive Director of the Steamboat Era Museum in Irvington, Virginia. She teaches graphic design at the University of Maryland University College.

Like Mike and his classmates, Barb is also celebrating a fiftieth anniversary. In 1964 she graduated from Edward Devotion Elementary School in Brookline, Massachusetts.

1964 Techmila Yearbook courtesy of
Ronald and Cheryl Mihills/RIT 1965